Cross Hedgehog

'aw' and 'au'

paw

saw

autumn

Summer was over. Autumn leaves were falling from the trees. They were in heaps around the garden wall.

Jelly was next to the wall. She was watching two birds on the grass. All of a sudden she heard a noise. 'Grr, grr.'

She looked around. She heard the noise again.

'Grr, grr.' It was coming from a heap of leaves next to the wall.

Jelly moved the leaves with her paw. She saw two noses. She heard the growling noise again. 'Grr, grr.'

The noise was coming from two big hedgehogs. They were getting the leaves in a heap ready for their winter sleep.

They were cross with Jelly, but she went on her way across the grass. Suddenly she cried, 'meow, meow.'

She looked down and saw some spikes in her paw. Then she saw a little hedgehog. She had trodden on it. It growled at her. 'Grr, grr'.

The little hedgehog was not hurt. Jelly said sorry to it. It growled again. 'Grr, grr.' The two big hedgehogs heard the noise.

They rushed out from their heap of leaves and ran towards Jelly and the little hedgehog. Jelly jumped on the garden wall.

She was safe from the cross hedgehogs. They growled at her. 'Grr, grr.' Jelly stayed away from their heap of leaves all winter.

Vowels:

ai/ay/a-e:	again away way stayed safe
ee/ea:	sleep trees heaps leaves
ie/i-e:	cried spikes
o/o-e:	over noses
oo:	looked
ow/ou:	down growling growled meow around out
ar:	garden
er:	summer winter over
er/ear:	her heard
ir:	birds
ur:	hurt
oi:	noise
aw/au:	paw saw autumn
ea:	ready
soft g:	hedgehogs
-y:	Jelly sorry suddenly

Verbs:

-ed verbs:	moved growled rushed stayed cried looked jumped
Others:	was were heard saw went said ran

Exceptions: they watching two their some towards coming